THE
LIBRARY OF **BATS**™

HORSESHOE BATS

EMILY RAABE

The Rosen Publishing Group's
PowerKids Press™
New York

For Lawrence M. Francis, with love

Published in 2003 by The Rosen Publishing Group, Inc.
29 East 21st Street, New York, NY 10010

First Edition

Editor: Natashya Wilson
Book Design: Emily Muschinske

Photo Credits: Cover and title page, pp. 5, 10, 11, 15 (inset), 16, 17 (bottom left), 18, 19, 21 © Merlin D. Tuttle, Bat Conservation International; p. 4 © B. G. Thomson/ANT Photo Library; pp. 6, 17 (top left, bottom right) © P. Laycock/American Society of Mammalogists, Mammal Images Library; p. 7 © G. D. Anderson/ANT Photo Library; p. 9 (top) © M. Andera/American Society of Mammalogists, Mammal Images Library; p. 9 (bottom) Eric De Palo; p. 12 © D. Whittford/ANT Photo Library; p. 12 (inset) © G. B. Baker/ANT Photo Library; pp. 13, 22 © R. Herd/American Society of Mammalogists, Mammal Images Library; p. 15 © Digital Stock; p. 17 (top right) © R. K. LaVal/American Society of Mammalogists, Mammal Images Library.

Raabe, Emily.
Horseshoe bats / Emily Raabe.
    p. cm. — (The library of bats)
Includes bibliographical references (p.   ).
Summary: An introduction to the appearance, behavior, and habitat of horseshoe bats, each of which has a U-shaped fold of skin called a nose-leaf.
ISBN 0-8239-6327-6 (lib. bdg.)
1. Horseshoe bats—Juvenile literature. [1. Horseshoe bats. 2. Bats.] I. Title.
QL737.C58 R224 2003
599.4—dc21
                                    2001007253

Manufactured in the United States of America

CONTENTS

BATS ARE NOT MICE!

What is a bat? Bats might look like furry mice with wings, but bats are not mice. Like mice, bats are **mammals**. Mammals have hair and backbones, and they feed their babies milk. Unlike mice, bats do not have front teeth that always grow. Bats are also different from mice and all other mammals in one important way. They are the only mammals that can fly. These amazing mammals live almost everywhere on Earth. Today scientists separate bats into 17 groups called **families**. Scientists know of 11 bat families that existed 50 million years ago. Of these 11 families, 5 became **extinct**, and 6 still exist today. The horseshoe bats make up one of these six families.

All horseshoe bats have horseshoe-shaped noses. This horseshoe bat has cloaked itself in its wings to get some rest. Its nose can be seen between its wings. ➡

BAT FACT

The German word for bat means "fluttering mouse." The French word means "bald mouse." Norwegians call a bat a "flying mouse," and one of the Chinese words for bat means "fairy rat." It's clear from these names that for many years, people thought that bats were simply mice with wings!

The Bat with the Horseshoe Nose

There are 69 **species**, or kinds, of horseshoe bats in the horseshoe bat family. Horseshoe bats come in many sizes and colors. They can weigh from ½ to 1 ounce (4–28 g). They can be red, brown, reddish brown, gray, or black. The one thing that all horseshoe bats have in common is the shape of their noses. Every horseshoe bat has folds of skin called a nose leaf. The lower part of a horseshoe bat's nose leaf is shaped like the letter *U*, or a horseshoe. This is how the bats got their name. The upper part of the nose leaf is thin and pointed, like a spear. It sticks out from the bat's face.

Bat Fact

Horseshoe bats have wide, broad wings with rounded ends. When they fly, they flutter and float like butterflies. This slow, fluttering flight allows horseshoe bats to fly slowly over the ground as they hunt for insects to eat.

Horseshoe bats have very small eyes that are partly covered by their nose leaves. This tells scientists that vision is not very important to horseshoe bats. They also have large ears, which means that hearing is very important to them.

OLD WORLD BATS

Some scientists divide the world into two sections, known as the New World and the Old World. The Old World is made up of Australia, Africa, Europe, and Asia. The New World is made up of North America, Central America, and South America. If you look on a map, you will see that the Old World is in the eastern half of the world, and the New World is in the western half. There are only three families of bats that live in both the New World and the Old World. These three families are the plain-nosed bats, the sheath-tailed bats, and the free-tailed bats. Six families of bats live only in the New World. Eight families, including horseshoe bats, live only in the Old World. Horseshoe bats live in Europe, Africa, Asia, and Australia.

BAT STATS

Plain-nosed bats live in both the New World and the Old World. They are the largest family of bats in the world. There are 355 species of plain-nosed bats! They are the most common bats in Europe and North America.

This map shows where horseshoe bats live in the Old World. They can live in areas that are colder than the areas in which many other bats can live.

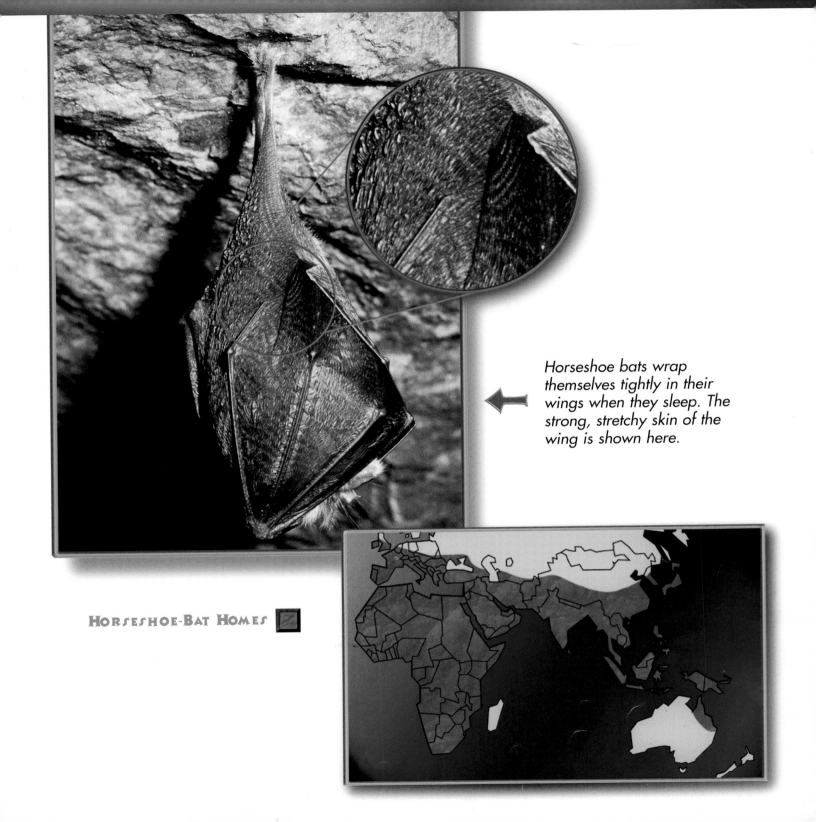

Horseshoe bats wrap themselves tightly in their wings when they sleep. The strong, stretchy skin of the wing is shown here.

HORSESHOE-BAT HOMES

Where Does a Horseshoe Bat Sleep?

Many types of bats crowd into their roost spaces. Horseshoe bats, on the other hand, usually do not hang close enough to touch one another. Even when it is cold, they do not snuggle together. Each bat has its own space in which it hangs, all wrapped up and cozy inside its blanket made of wings.

Horseshoe bats **roost** during the day in caves, in hollow trees, and in buildings. Sometimes they hang by one leg! Horseshoe bats that live in northern areas **hibernate** during the winter. Hibernation is a kind of deep sleep. Food is hard to find in the winter. Hibernation helps the bats to save energy and to stay alive until spring. Horseshoe bats need to hibernate in dark, wet caves so that they do not **dehydrate** while they are sleeping. The adults lose up to 20 percent of their body weight while hibernating. The young bats lose up to 30 percent. The hibernating bats grow weak and should not be disturbed.

Sometimes water droplets form on a hibernating bat. This helps to keep the bat from losing too much water.

Dinner for a Horseshoe Bat

Horseshoe bats leave their roosts after sundown to hunt for spiders and insects. Once they catch their **prey**, the bats will eat while flying. If its prey is large, a bat may go back to the roost to eat. Then it will fly off again to hunt some more. Horseshoe bats have different ways of catching their food. They pluck up insects from the ground. This is called **gleaning**. They also fly around and grab insects in the air. This is called **aerial hawking**. Sometimes they sit on a branch and wait for insects to fly by. When one does, the bat leaves its perch and catches the insect. This is called **flycatching**.

Bat Fact

Human beings can bend their necks in order to look up, down, and from side to side. Bats can bend their necks to look straight back behind them! They do this as they hang upside down by arching their backs and tilting their heads backward. This means that a roosting bat can still look all around for insects that might fly by.

This young horseshoe bat (top) is about to fly from its roost. The orange horseshoe bat (inset) arches its back and lifts its head to look behind its back.

FLYING IN THE DARK

As do most bats, horseshoe bats hunt in the dark of night. How do they see to hunt? In the 1790s, an Italian scientist named Lazarro Spallanzani decided to figure out the secret to bats' night flight. Spallanzani put a bat and an owl in a dark room, lit only with a candle. Both the bat and the owl flew around easily by candlelight. Spallanzani blew out the candle, making the room totally dark. The owl bumped into things. The bat flew around the room with no trouble. Spallanzani never figured out why. In the 1930s, American scientist Donald Griffin discovered that flying bats were sending out sounds as they flew. When the sound bounced off an object, the bats listened to the echo. This echo told them where the object was. Griffin called this **echolocation**.

BAT STATS

When bats echolocate, they need to be able to hear the echo with both ears. With 1 ear plugged, a bat will not be able to figure out from where the echo is coming. It will become confused.

A bat (inset) sends out a sound and listens for the echo to bounce back. Dolphins also use echolocation.

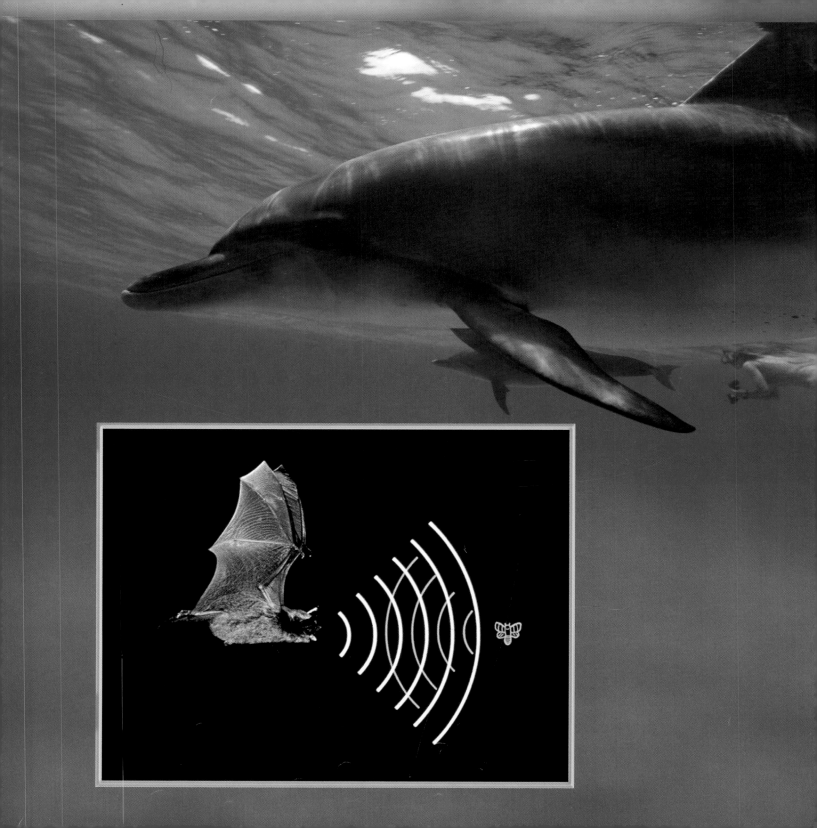

How Horseshoe Bats Hunt

Horseshoe bats use echolocation to hunt. They echolocate differently from many other bats. Most bats echolocate through their mouths. Horseshoe bats echolocate through their noses. Their nose leaves help them to direct sound, much as your hands direct sound when you cup them around your mouth to call to someone. Bats echolocate to find or to avoid objects. Horseshoe bats also echolocate to sense movement. They can find a flying insect by the fluttering of its wings. This makes them great at hunting in the dark, but if an insect stops moving, a horseshoe bat can no longer tell it's an insect.

BAT FACT

There are other bat families that echolocate through their noses. All of the bats in these families have fancy nose leaves on their faces, as do horseshoe bats. These other families include the false vampire bats (above), the Old World leaf-nosed bats, and the slit-faced bats.

As do horseshoe bats, Old World leaf-nosed bats, triple nose-leaf bats, and African trident-nosed bats have fancy nose leaves. They all echolocate through their nose.

OLD WORLD LEAF-NOSED BAT

TRIPLE NOSE-LEAF BAT

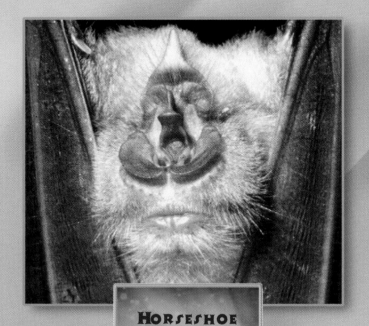

HORSESHOE BAT

AFRICAN TRIDENT-NOSED BAT

HILDEBRAND'S HORSESHOE BATS

Hildebrand's horseshoe bats are the biggest horseshoe bats in the world. They weigh from ⅞ to 1 ¼ ounces (25–35 g). These big bats have wide, broad wings that help them to fly slowly and to **hover** over an area while they search for insects. Hildebrand's horseshoe bats live only in eastern Africa. It is very hot there, so they do not need to hibernate. They live in caves, in hollow trees, and in the attics of buildings. They sometimes live in holes left by aardvarks or warthogs. Hildebrand's horseshoe bats like to hunt on the edges of forests, near rivers. They often stay out all night to hunt.

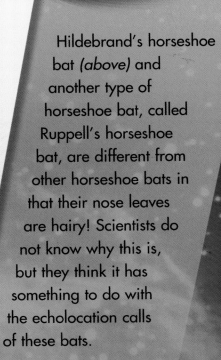

BAT FACT

Hildebrand's horseshoe bat (above) and another type of horseshoe bat, called Ruppell's horseshoe bat, are different from other horseshoe bats in that their nose leaves are hairy! Scientists do not know why this is, but they think it has something to do with the echolocation calls of these bats.

Hildebrand's horseshoe bats hunt by flycatching and by hovering close to the ground to catch low-flying insects. This Hildebrand's horseshoe bat has caught a moth.

Greater and Lesser Horseshoe Bats

Greater horseshoe bats are some of the largest horseshoe bats. Lesser horseshoe bats are some of the smallest. Greater horseshoe bats live in Great Britain, western and southern Europe, and India. They are about the size of pears. Lesser horseshoe bats are tiny bats that live in Great Britain, Europe, Asia, and northern Africa. They are only about the size of a small plum. Greater horseshoe bat babies are born gray and turn reddish brown as they grow up. Lesser horseshoe bat babies are born a darker gray. The adults look like small greater horseshoe bats, except their fur is a grayish brown color. Both greater and lesser horseshoe bats eat beetles, moths, and flies.

Bat Stats

Lesser horseshoe bats can live for about 21 years. Greater horseshoe bats can live for 30 years! However, both types of bats usually live only from 3 to 7 years.

Greater horseshoe bats (left) weigh about four times as much as lesser horseshoe bats (right).

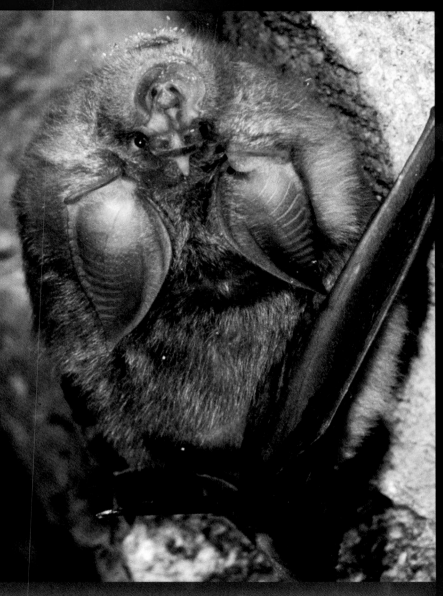

GREATER HORSESHOE BAT

Where Have the Horseshoe Bats Gone?

The **populations** of horseshoe bats have grown smaller throughout the world. This happens for many reasons. Houses are built on land where the bats like to hunt. Some horseshoe bats die when people accidentally disturb bats' roosting sites or purposely kill the bats. The bats also die when they eat insects that have been poisoned with **insecticides**. In Great Britain, the greater horseshoe bat population has gone down 90 percent since 1900. In 1981, the British government passed the Wildlife and Countryside Act. This act makes it **illegal** to disturb bats in Great Britain. It is hoped that acts such as this will help horseshoe bats and all bats to survive a little longer.

Bat Fact

Horseshoe bats must not be disturbed while they are hibernating. If people enter a cave where horseshoe bats are hibernating, the bats will wake up and fly away. They may even search for a new hibernation spot. This much activity in the middle of winter has caused the death of thousands of these bats.

Glossary

aerial hawking (EHR-ee-uhl HAHK-ing) Catching insects that are in the air while flying.

dehydrate (dee-HY-drayt) To lose too much water.

echolocation (eh-koh-loh-KAY-shun) A method of locating objects by producing a sound and judging the time it takes the echo to return and the direction from which it returns. Bats, dolphins, porpoises, killer whales, and some shrews all use echolocation.

extinct (ik-STINKT) No longer in existence. Died out.

families (FAM-leez) Scientific names for groups of plants or animals that are alike in some ways.

flycatching (FLY-kach-ing) Waiting in one place for an insect to fly by, then chasing and catching it.

gleaning (GLEEN-ing) Catching insects that are on the ground while flying.

hibernate (HY-bur-nayt) To spend the winter in a sleeplike state, with heart rate and breathing slowed down.

hover (HUH-ver) To stay in one place while still staying airborn.

illegal (ih-LEE-gul) Against the law.

insecticides (in-SEHK-tih-sydz) Harmful substances used to kill insects.

mammals (MA-mulz) Warm-blooded animals that have backbones and hair, breathe air, and feed milk to their young.

populations (pah-pyoo-LAY-shunz) Numbers of animals living in certain areas.

prey (PRAY) An animal that is hunted by another animal for food.

roost (ROOST) A place where bats or birds sleep.

species (SPEE-sheez) A single kind of plant or animal. Humans are one species.

INDEX

WEB SITES

Due to the changing nature of Internet links, PowerKids Press has developed an online list of Web sites related to the subject of this book. This site is updated regularly. Please use this link to access the list: www.powerkidslinks.com/lob/horsho/